197
'UM

Traverse City, MI 49685-1108

SAILING THE HIGH SEAS

SAILING THE HIGH SEAS

Henry Humphrey

David McKay Company, Inc.
New York

Library of Congress Cataloging in Publication Data

Humphrey, Henry, 1930-
  Sailing the high seas.

  SUMMARY: Describes the 12-day voyage of four
crew members aboard a ketch from Oriental, N.C., across
the Atlantic Ocean to the Caribbean island of Antigua.
  1. Sailing—Juvenile literature. [1. Sailing]
I. Title.
GV811.H83.   797.1'24   79-2113
ISBN 0-679-20953-0

1 2 3 4 5 6 7 8 9 10
Manufactured in the United States of America

This is for Maud Gonne Humphrey, who used to be "Squeaky." With love from her adoring father.

ACKNOWLEDGMENTS

I was incredibly lucky to find myself sailing with an extraordinary group of people: Naomi Kramer, Jack Maury, and Roger Wing. All three are experienced sailors and they were very patient when cameras were trained on them. Jack and Roger have given me an immeasurable amount of information and a feel of the sea. My fellow crew members and friends have my gratitude. And I'd like to also thank Mr. Henry Straus, owner of the *Doki*—a comfortable and very seaworthy boat. Mr. Allen Rogers, of Whitby Boat Works Ltd., kindly supplied useful information about the structural details of the *Doki*.

SAILING THE HIGH SEAS

Foreword

Supposing somebody called you up and asked if you would like to sail across the ocean in a small boat (not too small), wouldn't you be excited?

Sailing The High Seas will re-create that experience for you. You'll get an idea of what an oceangoing sailboat is like, inside and out. You'll find out how members of the boat's crew spend their days and nights on board. You'll also find out what it's like to be at the wheel of the boat, as she crashes through the Atlantic Ocean on her way to the Caribbean and the island of Antigua.

Here you are at the helm, in Mid-Atlantic—crashing through seas driven by a 20 knot "breeze," on your way to the Caribbean and the island of Antigua, (pronounced "antee'ga"). The boat is heeling to starboard under the pressure of the wind on the sails. It feels as if you're doing about 50 miles an hour. Actually, the boat's top speed is about 7½–8 knots. You're now doing about 6.

Sailors have many terms for the sea and ships that are rarely heard on land. For example, a helm is a steering wheel attached to a boat's rudder. When a boat heels or is hove over, it means she is leaning away from the wind. Starboard is to the right, as you face the front, or bow, of the boat. The opposite of starboard is port, or left.

Knots of all kinds are important to sailors. However, knots also refer to the number of nautical miles traveled per hour. A nautical mile is 6,080.20 feet, or a little over 800 feet more than a land, or statute-mile of 5280 feet. Six knots, then, would be slightly under 7 miles an hour.

Now that you've had a bit of a preview of the trip, you should meet the rest of the crew: Naomi, Roger, and Jack. You'll get to know each other pretty well during the voyage.

You should also get to know the boat. Named the *Doki* (a Dutch term of endearment), she was built in 1974 (boats are always called "she"—nobody knows why). *Doki*, a Whitby 42, was built by the Whitby Boat Works Ltd. in Ontario, Canada. Her length on deck is 42 feet. The *Doki* is rigged as a ketch, meaning that she has two masts. The taller mast is the mainmast, and it carries the mainsail and a variety of jibs, which are usually smaller than the mainsail. The shorter mast aft (toward the back, or stern) of the helm is called the mizzenmast. It carries the mizzen sail.

Opposite:
(*Courtesy Robert K. Berry Assoc.*)

The picture of a Whitby 42 (not the *Doki*) shows from left to right, the different sails:

1. Jib (it happens to be a Genoa jib, which is larger than an ordinary jib and, therefore, will give the boat more speed than an ordinary jib would. There are times when the wind is blowing too hard and a smaller jib would be better to use.)
2. The mainsail. Sailors usually pronounce that "main'sul," just as they say "main' mist" for mainmast.
3. The "mizzen'sul" or "mizzen" is actually a mizzen sail.

Now you can see what the cabins below deck look like. There are three cabins where the crew sleep: the after cabin (in the stern of the boat), the midship cabin and the forward cabin. There are bunks for seven people. The forward water tank is located under the forward bunk. There is also a door to the chain locker in the forward cabin. The chain locker, which is really the inside of the bow, is where anchor rope and a spare anchor are kept. Anchors used to have chains, but now ropes are used.

After cabin.

Midships cabin.

Forward cabin.

Forward water tank.

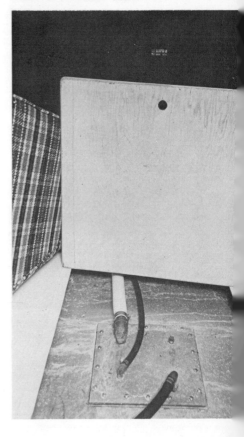

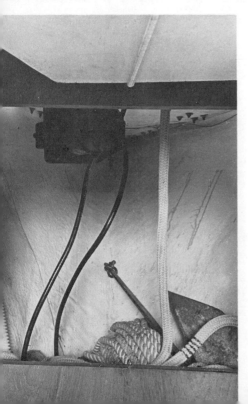

Chain locker.

The "head" is a bathroom which has a toilet equipped with a hand pump to flush it with sea water. The sink has two faucets—one that works with an electric pump and one that is worked by hand. There are two heads on board.

Head.

The faucets on the galley, or kitchen, sink work the same way as in the heads. With the one that is powered by the electric pump, all you have to do is turn it on. To get water out of the faucets worked by hand, you have to pump the handle from left to right. Who needs this kind of faucet? Everybody on board does if the electric pump breaks down.

Because you're about to leave on a trip across 1400 miles of ocean, you have to take on supplies of food, water, and fuel to last the estimated two weeks at sea. It's a good idea to add food for another week or two, in case there are unexpected delays, such as no wind and the boat's engine breaking down.

The *Doki* is equipped with a refrigerator and a freezer, so you can bring on fresh and frozen meat, vegetables, and fruit in addition to canned goods. Because refrigerators are not always the most reliable equipment on a boat, it's important to have enough canned food to last the entire trip. If it's not eaten, it will still be good for future trips.

Water faucet–electric pump.

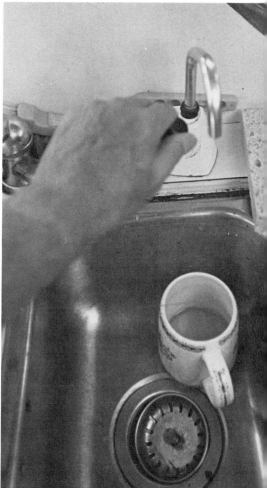

Starting the pumping action
for the manual faucet.

You have to make sure that the three fuel tanks are full. Today, it takes only 26.8 gallons of diesel fuel to fill the tanks. Two of them hold 65 gallons each and one holds 90 gallons—a total of 220 gallons. The *Doki's* 80-horsepower diesel engine uses about one gallon per hour when running. The

Fuel pump dial face.

engine turns a propeller that moves the boat through the water at approximately 6 knots. The engine also runs two alternators that generate electricity. One alternator supplies power for the refrigerator and freezer. The other charges the two large 12-volt storage batteries which, in turn, supply electricity for all the lights and the pumps on board. Even when there is plenty of wind, the engine is run an hour or two every day just to keep the refrigerator and freezer cool and to charge the batteries.

One of the pumps supplies water pressure for the faucets in the galley sink and in the two heads. The other one pumps water out of the bilge area below the floor boards. The best of boats leak a small amount of salt water into the bilges. After awhile, the water accumulates, and it has to be pumped out through a hole in the side of the boat. The boat won't leak through this hole because the pipe carrying the bilge water to the hole is made in such a way that it allows the water to flow only to the outside of the boat.

In addition to fuel, you must also fill your three water tanks with fresh water. These tanks have about the same capacity as the fuel tanks. When all the tanks are filled with water or fuel, you have added about one and one-half tons to the total weight of the boat. When empty, she weighs 12 tons. This additional weight affects the way the Doki sails. Because it keeps her lower in the water, the hull is less affected by the wind. The full water tank in the forward cabin tends to keep the bow in the water when sailing in heavy seas, making the Doki a bit easier to steer.

Equally important is fuel for the crew. It takes a lot of skill for Naomi to be able to stow groceries (stores) for three or four weeks in the available spaces—under seats and even under the floor boards—in this case right around the bilge pump.

Naomi
stowing
the stores.

Food is stored around the bilge pump.

The *Doki*, tied up.

Of course, all the provisioning of the boat is done while the *Doki* is tied up to a dock, or "slip," at our point of departure: Oriental, North Carolina. Because she's tied up, you can see the main anchor secured to the bow. It's called a plow anchor due to the way it looks and because it plows its way into the bottom and holds the boat very well.

13

Two weeks earlier, the boat had been moved to North Carolina from Connecticut because, at this time of year, the North Atlantic can be very rough. It's November 6th, but, as the Carolina sun climbs, so does the temperature. It's clear and sunny, and the thermometer registers in the 70s at noon.

By 4:00 P.M., the *Doki* is fully loaded with food, fuel, and water. The time has come to begin your trip, or "get underway." Roger casts off all the ropes, or lines, from the slip. The engine is started and is shifted into reverse at "dead slow" speed. You'll run on the engine until you are in the open Atlantic because the *Doki* needs room to sail. The boat backs out of the slip, turns, and heads toward the Intercoastal Waterway (it looks like a canal) which, in turn, will lead you to the Atlantic.

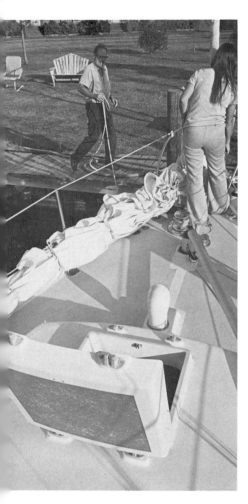

Casting off.

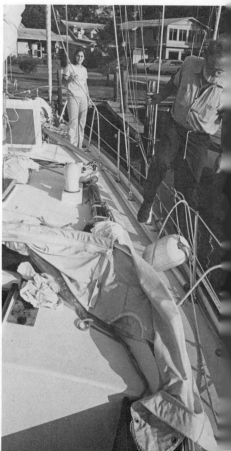

In reverse, dead slow.

Watch for the buoys.

Now you'll have to keep a sharp watch for the buoys that mark the channel for the approach to the Intercoastal Waterway. If you miss the channel, the *Doki*, which draws 5 feet 4 inches, will surely become stuck in the mud. This could delay the trip for many hours until she is towed off the mud.

When sailors say that a boat draws 5 feet 4 inches, they mean that the bottom of the boat, including the keel, extends 5 feet 4 inches below the surface of the water. Incidentally, the keel is like a large fin that extends from the bottom of the boat. On the *Doki*, the keel stretches from the propeller two-thirds of the way to the bow. It's weighted to help stabilize the boat. All sailboats must have a keel, or something very much like it, to keep the boat from slipping sideways when sailing close to the wind.

Intercoastal Waterway.

You have found your way safely into the Waterway. It's a beautiful place in the dreamlike evening. Enormous birds—great blue herons—squawk at the boat's approach, then fly to a safe distance to watch the *Doki* pass.

By the time you are through the Waterway and pass Moorehead City, North Carolina, the sun has long ago set. As you motor into the Atlantic, the last sight you'll have of the United States is the lights of North Carolina's Atlantic Beach receding from the *Doki*'s stern.

Now that you are on the high seas—completely out of sight of land—it might be a good idea to look at the chart to find out the best course to sail.

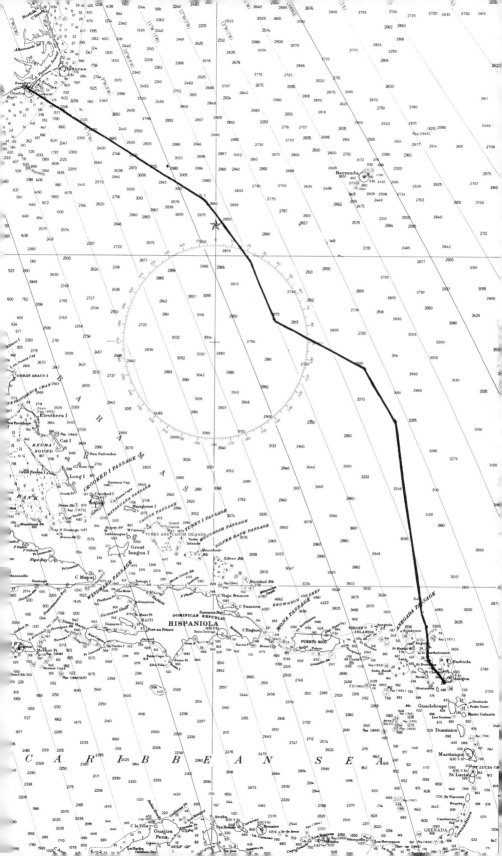

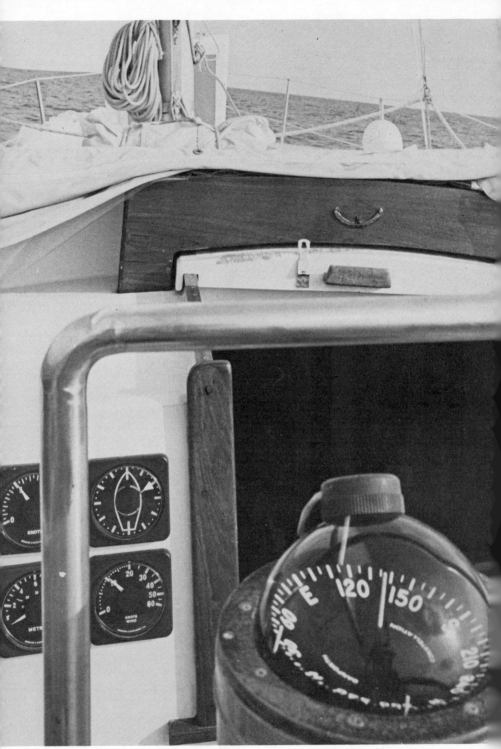

Sailing a course of 120°.

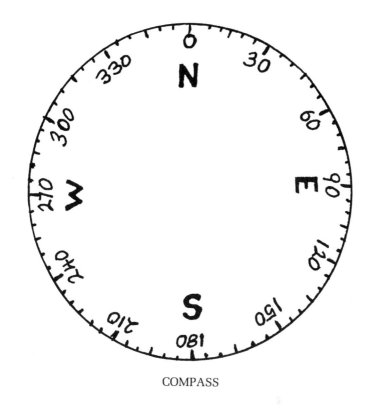

COMPASS

We'll sail a little south of east (120°) for about 600 miles (those are nautical miles; any mention of miles in this book will mean nautical miles). The reason for the easterly course is that somewhere between 600 and 700 miles on a course of 120° will get the boat into the northeast trade winds. Trade winds blow from the northeast above the equator and from the southwest below the equator. The word "trade" is an old nautical word meaning course or track. Since these winds blow continually on the same course, they are known as trade winds. Once the *Doki* arrives in the trade winds the course will be changed to 180°, or due south.

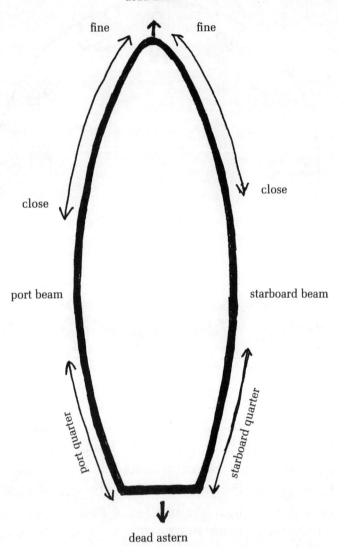

PORT BOW   STARBOARD BOW

dead ahead

fine   fine

close   close

port beam   starboard beam

port quarter   starboard quarter

dead astern

When you get into the trade winds, it should be
an easy sail—going due south with the wind coming
off your "port quarter." The drawing will show you
how sailors call directions from the boat. But long

22

before you get to the trade winds, about the second day out from North Carolina, you'll cross into one of the miracles of the oceans: that enormous current of warm water, called the Gulf Stream, flowing from the Gulf of Mexico.

This is your second morning at sea. As you steer your course, you will notice that the color of the water is beginning to change from gray-green to dark blue.

Jack puts a bucket over the side to scoop up some of the water. Its temperature is 72°. The temperature of the water off Atlantic Beach, North Carolina, was about 60°. You have now crossed into the Gulf Stream. You'll have to steer a little bit further south here just to hold your course because the Gulf Stream is a strong current, flowing in a northeasterly direction. It has a far-reaching effect on the weather, not only where you are sailing, but also as far away as England and Ireland. Because of the Gulf Stream, palm trees grow in southwestern Ireland, although it is on the same latitude as Newfoundland and Labrador.

Jack puts a bucket over the side.

The temperature confirms it.

The breeze is picking up. You scan the four instruments in front of you at the helm. The first (reading clockwise from the top left) tells you your speed in knots. That instrument is called a log. There is a small propeller under the boat (it has nothing to do with the engine), which turns as the boat drags it through the water. That motion is recorded on the log dial.

The next instrument shows from which direction the wind is hitting the sails. That's not as obvious as it seems. Because of the forward motion of the boat, the wind will seem to be coming from ahead even if it is actually coming from off the port beam.

The bottom right instrument indicates how fast the wind is blowing.

The next dial, when it's on, shows the depth of the water. Since you are now sailing in water approximately 10,000 feet deep, there is not much need for the depth gauge, which registers a maximum of 195 feet. You'll probably use it when you approach land and start looking for channels.

There's one thing about sailing on the high seas that's different from going out for a one-day sail: The boat must be sailed 24 hours a day. Obviously, this would be difficult for one person to do (although it has been done many times—usually with the help of an automatic steering device). So, a schedule of watches, or "watch bill," is worked out. You and the other members of the crew total four people. Each person must have an equal amount of time on watch.

Opposite:
Scan the four instruments in front of you.

The person on watch is responsible for keeping the boat on course. Here's a sample watch bill for Sunday, Monday, Tuesday, and Wednesday:

WATCH BILL FOR THE KETCH *Doki*

Hours:	Sunday	Monday	Tuesday	Wednesday
2400–0200	1	3	1	3
0200–0400	2	4	2	4
0400–0600	3	1	3	1
0600–0800	4	2	4	2
0800–1100	1	3	1	3
1100–1400	2	4	2	4
1400–1700	3	1	3	1
1700–2000	4	2	4	2
2000–2200	1	3	1	3
2200–2400	2	4	2	4

Key: 1 = Jack, 2 = Naomi, 3 = Roger, 4 = you

On boats, 24-hour time is used: 2400 is midnight; 0200 is two o'clock in the morning, and so on until 1200, which is noon. Then 1400 is 2 P.M.; 1700 is 5 P.M. and so forth.

A similar schedule must also be worked out so that everyone can take an equal number of turns in the galley, prepare meals for the crew, and then wash the dishes.

You'll notice there is something that looks like a little cap on the back of the lens over the compass. The cap contains a light bulb behind a deep red filter. At night, the compass glows a deep red color. That way your vision of the dark waters around you won't be destroyed by a bright light.

The little cap on the back of the lens, over the compass.

Watching for other ships.

The person on watch is also responsible for watching out for other ships. The Gulf Stream includes a major commercial shipping lane, and you'll probably see several large ships. You must watch out for them, even though a boat under sail always has the right of way over a ship under power, no matter how large the ship is. However, it takes a large ship miles to change course, and the *Doki*, although in the right, would probably not survive a collision with a merchant ship.

All merchant, or commercial, ships are equipped with radar. A sailboat, even as big or bigger than the *Doki*, is almost invisible on radar unless her sails are wet. Wet sails improve the reflection of radar signals. The sails will be wet only if it is raining or the seas are very heavy. Therefore, a radar reflector is suspended between the *Doki*'s main and mizzenmasts in the hope that any large ship seeing a "blip," or reflection, on the radar screen will then steer away from it.

If you are under sail and you have to make a sudden change in course, you will have to change the position of your sails. In an emergency, if you head into the wind, you'll stop. But, you won't want to stay that way long—especially if there is a current and a heavy sea running. When you are stopped, you can no longer steer the boat. The rudder, which is attached to the wheel (helm), only influences the course of the boat when she is moving.

Radar reflector.

A monotonous job.

The person at the helm, who is on watch, has the responsibility for the whole boat and everyone in it. There are times, though, when this can be a boring job. You can also become hypnotized by the compass, particularly if you happen to be on the 0400 to 0600 watch.

The Atlantic gets rough.

Foul weather gear.

The trick is for the cook to stay in the galley.

But, it's never boring when the Atlantic is rough. Then, you put on your "foul weather gear," or rain suit. This consists of a hat, jacket, and trousers, usually made out of nylon, and water-proofed with a coating of vinyl or rubber. The hat is called a "sou'wester" because bad weather, including heavy rain, often comes from the southwest of England. There are also special boating shoes, with fine, wavy treads on the rubber soles that give you as good a footing as possible on wet decks. If it's not too cold, just plain feet give a good grip on the *Doki's* deck. Just watch out for stubbed toes!

Even when the weather is bad, life on the *Doki* goes on. The crew has to eat. But the pitching and rolling of the boat make things difficult for the cook. The stove, however, swings freely, so that it is level no matter what the boat is doing. But, the cook (Jack) must stay in the galley and not roll back and forth across the floor—a very easy thing to do!

There are
magnificent
sunsets.

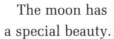

The moon has
a special beauty.

The weather on the Atlantic isn't always foul. There are magnificent sunsets, and even the moon has a special beauty over a smooth, shining sea.

34

You and the *Doki* are making progress. You're also in extremely deep waters—2 to 4 miles deep. You are sailing through the legendary and mysterious Sargasso Sea. Sargasso is the Portugese word for seaweed, and you can see clumps of it floating by. At times, masses of the weed clump together. The sight of these masses used to terrify sailors, who believed that the huge quantity of weed would ensnare their ship and drag it to the bottom. They also thought that the clumps of weed were inhabited by sea monsters. Until very recently, it was believed that the seaweed could also foul the propellers of ships. Where does the weed come from? When Columbus sailed into the Sargasso Sea, he was afraid the weed was attached to rocks just under the surface, so he took soundings by tossing a weighted line over the side to measure the distance to the bottom. Because the water is so deep, it became obvious that the weed couldn't grow on the bottom of the Sea. For a long time, scientists thought it was seaweed which originally grew near the islands of the West Indies, and that it had been torn up by the wind and rough seas. But, the seaweed growing near the islands was found to be unlike the seaweed in the Sargasso Sea. Sargasso weed is a species of brown algae, called "gulfweed." It does not come from coastal regions but has adapted to the open sea. It reproduces by division, and is supported by tiny air sacs that look like beads. You can see one or two of the air sacs in the closeup of the weed in one of the *Doki*'s glass cereal bowls..

The Sargasso Sea is not only deep, it's huge—about 2 million square miles, and the *Doki* is sailing

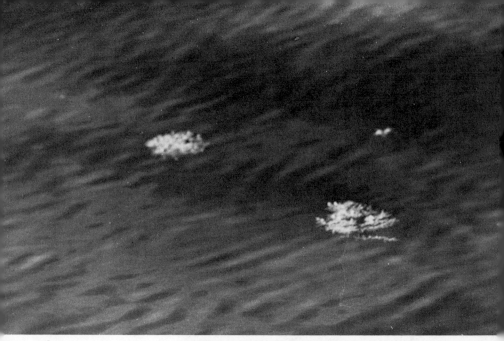

Clumps of seaweed.

A close-up
of Sargasso
Sea seaweed.

right through the middle of it. The water is an unusually deep blue, and is very clear. When a white disk, 6 feet in diameter, was once lowered 200 feet below the surface, it could be seen clearly. The reason why the water is so clear is because of its great depth, the absence of islands, and the great distance from any continents that might make the water muddy. There is also very little plankton, the miniature sea creatures that large fish feed upon. Where there is a great deal of plankton, the water is cloudy.

When the seas are calm, the crew catches up on some necessary work. Jack sews a patch on the main boom vang. The boom is the long pole which is attached to, and is perpendicular to, the mast. The bottom of the mainsail, or the mizzen sail, is attached to a boom. The vang is used to keep the main boom from constantly swinging back and forth when there is very little breeze and the engine is on. The mainsail is set to stabilize the boat, or to keep it from rolling too much in "swells"—long, old waves which originate in storms hundreds of miles away.

Jack sews a patch.

One thing we haven't talked about yet is how you know where you're going. There are no sign posts or buoys in mid-ocean, but the sun will tell you where you are with the help of a sextant. If you look into the sextant, you can see the sun (through a heavy filter), and you can see the horizon. By adjusting the sextant, the sun is "moved" so that it seems to sit on the horizon. Numbers are read from the instrument, and the time of the sighting is recorded. With a certain amount of calculation, the position of the boat is determined. To ensure that the sextant will give you accurate results, it is important to know the exact time. Roger is setting the navigator's watch according to an extremely accurate time signal, broadcast by the U.S. Bureau of Standards from Fort Collins, Colorado, on a number of short wave radio bands. It would not be possible to teach you the complicated subject of navigation in this book, but you may be sure that it works and that our position is correct to within five miles. Because the navigator has determined that the *Doki* has steered east far enough, we will change course to due south, or 180°. Light trade winds fill the sails. And, to get the most out of the wind, a huge jib, called a flasher, is set to give the *Doki* added speed in the light breeze. The flasher is set in addition to the Genoa jib already there. As you can see, the flasher is set outside, or forward, of the Genoa jib, known as a "Jenny." Jack is hauling on the flasher halyard to get the top of the giant jib all the way to the masthead (the top of the mast). Then, with a booming sound, it "breaks out," or opens almost like a parachute. The third picture in the series shows

Looking into the sextant.

The numbers are read off the instrument.

The *Doki*'s position is determined.

Roger sets the navigator's watch.

Change course to due south.

Hauling on the flasher halyard.

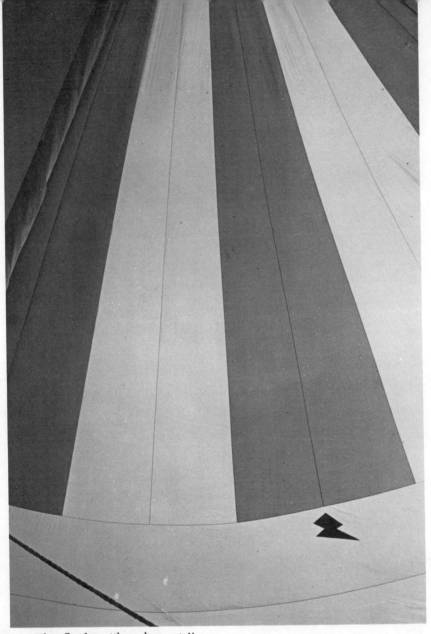

The flasher "breaks out."

Jack making the flasher halyard secure on a cleat—
an anvil-shaped device around which lines are
wrapped. The lines will stay secure, but they can be
quickly released from the cleat when that time
comes.

Making the flasher halyard secure on a cleat.

First, the swallow landed in the galley.

Just before departing through an open hatch.

Occasionally, strange things happen at sea. The *Doki* is at least 300 miles from any land, but a little land bird, a swallow, comes on board. First, he lands in the galley. Then, he lights on top of a closet, before he departs through an open hatch.

Hatches are used for ventilation and are important for that reason. It's almost impossible to get too much air below decks. But there are other ways of getting air below. There are ventilators, or air scoops, on deck, each about 8 inches in diameter, that force air through holes in the cabin ceiling. However, the amount of air they put into a cabin is barely noticeable.

Hatches are for ventilation.

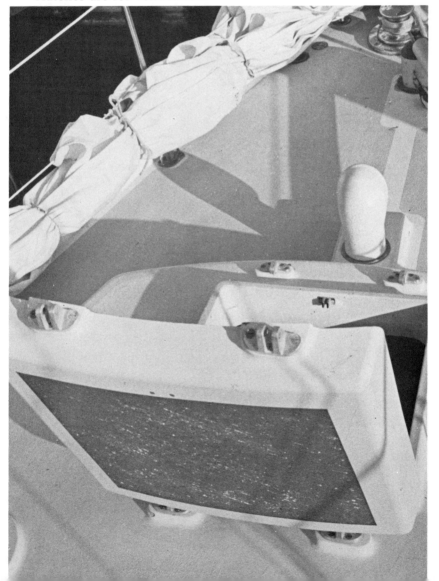

A flying fish next to a ventilator.

In the close-up picture, you may notice something unusual next to the ventilator. It happens to be a flying fish that hit the deck in the middle of the night with such force that some of its scales were knocked off. The little flying fish (7 to 8 inches long) try to escape from bigger fish that prey on them. They swim at great speed, break out of a wave, and glide on air currents created by the waves. They can fly for over a hundred feet, and they can make turns in mid-air before they come down. Their technique for survival must work, because they are found in tropical seas everywhere.

The *Doki* is getting closer to her destination, the island of Antigua. Roger, the navigator, hears coded radio signals from an automatic transmitter on the island. He hears the signals through a pair of earphones, connected to the radio direction finder in his hands. He tunes for the weakest signal because, at a distance, it's easier to tell when the signal is weakest. When he is certain the signals are the way they should be, Roger looks at the compass on top of the direction finder and sees the exact direction to Antigua. It's just a way of confirming his work with the sextant, because he can't be too sure of both the *Doki*'s position and the course she is sailing. Roger estimates arrival in Antigua the following day.

Turning the radio direction finder.

Trying to find the weakest signal.

Having found the weakest station, Roger reads the bearing of the radio station on the compass on top of the direction finder.

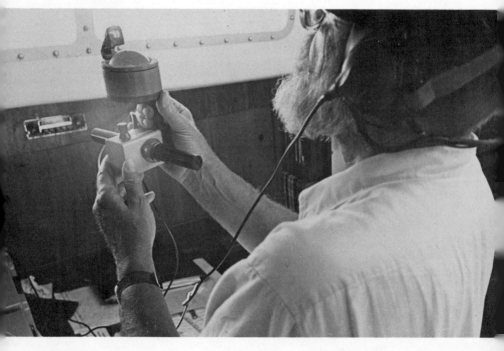

There it is! Antigua!

At dawn, Friday, November 17th, there it is! Antigua—under the rising tropical sun. It's the first land you've seen since the *Doki* left the United States twelve days ago. In five hours, you will anchor the boat in English Harbor. It's been a voyage of discovery, fun, and some excitement, but it will be good to set foot on solid land again.

Common Metric Equivalents and Conversions

Approximate

1 inch	= 25 millimeters
1 foot	= 30 centimeters
1 foot	= 0.3 meter
1 square mile	= 2.6 square kilometers
1 millimeter	= 0.04 inch
1 meter	= 3.3 feet
l square kilometer	= 0.4 square mile
1 pound	= 0.45 kilogram
1 short ton	= 0.9 metric ton
1 kilogram	= 2.2 pounds
1 metric ton	= 1.1 short tons
1 gallon	= 3.8 liters
1 liter	= 0.26 gallon

Temperature Conversion

The Celsius scale (C), often called the centigrade scale, is derived from the Fahrenheit scale by the following formula:

$$C = \frac{5\ (F - 32)}{9}$$

51